THE FLAGS OF THE UNION
AN ILLUSTRATED HISTORY

THE FLAGS OF THE UNION

AN ILLUSTRATED HISTORY

BY DEVEREAUX D. CANNON, JR.

PELICAN PUBLISHING COMPANY
Gretna 1994

The word "Pelican" and the depiction of a pelican are
trademarks of Pelican Publishing Company, Inc., and are
registered in the U.S. Patent and Trademark Office.

Library of Congress Cataloging-in-Publication Data

Cannon, Devereaux D., 1954-
    The flags of the Union : an illustrated history / Devereaux D.
Cannon, Jr.
       p. cm.
    Includes bibliographical references and index.
    ISBN 0-88289-953-8
    1. Flags—United States—History. 2. United States—History—
Civil War, 1861-1865—Flags. I. Title.
CR113.C366 1993
929.9'2'0973—dc20   93-22570
                                               CIP

Illustrations by Larry Pardue

Manufactured in Korea

Published by Pelican Publishing Company, Inc.
1101 Monroe Street, Gretna, Louisiana 70053

Contents

List of Illustrations 7

Preface 11

Introduction 13

Chapter 1   The Stars and Stripes 17

Chapter 2   The National Flag in the United States Army 25

       I   Garrison Flag 25

       II   Storm Flag 26

       III   Recruiting Flag 26

Chapter 3   Infantry Colors 29

       I   The National Color 29

       II   The Regimental Color 31

       III   Camp Colors 34

       IV   Flank and General Guide Markers 35

Chapter 4   Standards and Guidons of Cavalry Regiments 37

       I   The Standard 37

       II   Guidons 38

Chapter 5   Colors of Artillery Regiments 41

Chapter 6   The Medical Service 43

Chapter 7   Designating Flags 45

       I   Army of the Potomac 46

       II   Army of the James 58

       III   Army of the Cumberland 62

       IV   Army of the Ohio 73

Chapter 8   Naval Flags 75

       I   The National Ensign 76

       II   The Union Jack 77

       III   The Commission Pennant 78

       IV   Officers' Flags 78

       V   Signal Flags 80

       VI   Foreign Flags 81

       VII   Distribution of Flags to Naval Vessels 81

Chapter 9   Revenue Service Flags 83

Further Reading 85

Appendix A: United States Flag Laws 87
Appendix B: Revised Regulations for the Army of
      the United States 88
Appendix C: General Orders No. 4 90
Appendix D: Dimensions of Navy Ensigns,
      Pennants, Jacks, Etc 91
Index 94

List of Illustrations

Figure 1.   The British Red Ensign

Figure 2.   The Grand Union Flag

Figure 3.   The Stars and Stripes

Figure 4.   The "American Stripes"

Figure 5.   Flag of the United States, 1795 to 1818

Figure 6.   Flag Flown at the U.S. Capitol in 1817

Figure 7.   Flag of the United States, 1818 to 1819

Figure 8.   Flag of the United States, 1861 to 1863

Figure 9.   Flag of the United States, 1863 to 1865

Figure 10.   United States Army Garrison Flag, 1861 to 1863

Figure 11.   United States Army Storm Flag, 1863 to 1865

Figure 12.   United States Army Recruiting Flag, 1861 to 1863

Figure 13.   National Color of a U.S. Army Infantry Regiment

Figure 14.   National Color of a Pennsylvania Infantry Regiment with Battle Honors

Figure 15.   Regimental Color of a U.S. Army Infantry Regiment

Figure 16.   Regimental Color of a Regiment of the Irish Brigade

Figure 17.   Diagram of the Camp of an Infantry Regiment

Figure 18.   Camp Colors Authorized Prior to 1862

Figure 19.   Camp Colors after January 1862

Figure 20.   Standard of a U.S. Cavalry Regiment

Figure 21.   Regimental Standard of a Pennsylvania Cavalry Regiment

Figure 22.   U.S. Cavalry Guidon Prior to 1862

Figure 23.   U.S. Cavalry Guidon after January 1862

Figure 24.   Regimental Color of a U.S. Artillery Regiment

Figure 25.   U.S. Army Hospital Flag

Figure 26.   U.S. Medical Service Guidon

Figure 27.   General Grant's Headquarters Flag, 1864 to 1865

Figure 28.   Headquarters Flag of the Army of the Potomac, 1864 to 1865

Figure 29. Headquarters Flag of the First Corps, Army of the Potomac, 1863 to 1865

Figure 30. Pattern of Division Headquarters Flags, First Corps, Army of the Potomac

Figure 31. Headquarters Flag of the Second Corps, Army of the Potomac, 1864 to 1865

Figure 32. Pattern of Division Headquarters Flags, Second Corps, Army of the Potomac

Figure 33. Headquarters Flag of the Third Corps, Army of the Potomac, 1864 to 1865

Figure 34. Pattern of Division Headquarters Flags, Third Corps, Army of the Potomac

Figure 35. Headquarters Flag of the Fifth Corps, Army of the Potomac, 1864 to 1865

Figure 36. Pattern of Division Headquarters Flags, Fifth Corps, Army of the Potomac

Figure 37. Headquarters Flag of the Sixth Corps, Army of the Potomac, 1864 to 1865

Figure 38. Pattern of Division Headquarters Flags, Sixth Corps, Army of the Potomac

Figure 39. Headquarters Flag of the Ninth Corps, Army of the Potomac, 1864 to 1865

Figure 40. Pattern of Division Headquarters Flags, Ninth Corps, Army of the Potomac

Figure 41. Headquarters Flag of the Eleventh Corps, Army of the Potomac, 1864 to 1865

Figure 42. Pattern of Division Headquarters Flags, Eleventh Corps, Army of the Potomac

Figure 43. Headquarters Flag of the Twelfth Corps, Army of the Potomac, 1864 to 1865

Figure 44. Pattern of Division Headquarters Flags, Twelfth Corps, Army of the Potomac

Figure 45. Headquarters Flag of the Nineteenth Corps, Army of the Potomac, 1864 to 1865

Figure 46. Pattern of Division Headquarters Flags, Nineteenth Corps, Army of the Potomac

Figure 47. Headquarters Flag of the Twenty-Fourth Corps, Army of the Potomac, 1864 to 1865

Figure 48.   Pattern of Division Headquarters Flags, Twenty-Fourth Corps, Army of the Potomac

Figure 49.   Headquarters Flag of the Twenty-Fifth Corps, Army of the Potomac, 1864 to 1865

Figure 50.   Pattern of Division Headquarters Flags, Twenty-Fifth Corps, Army of the Potomac

Figure 51.   Headquarters Flag of the Cavalry Corps, Army of the Potomac, 1864 to 1865

Figure 52.   Pattern of Division Headquarters Flags, Cavalry Corps, Army of the Potomac

Figures 53.   Headquarters Flag of the Department of Virginia and North Carolina, 1864 to 1865

Figure 54.   Headquarters Flag of the Tenth Corps, Army of the James, 1864 to 1865

Figure 55.   Pattern for Headquarters Flag of the First Division, Tenth (White Stars on Blue Field) and Eighteenth (White Stars on Red Field) Corps, Army of the James

Figure 56.   Pattern for Headquarters Flag of the Second Division, Tenth (White Stars on Blue Field) and Eighteenth (White Stars on Red Field) Corps, Army of the James

Figure 57.   Pattern for Headquarters Flag of the Third Division, Tenth (White Stars on Blue Field) and Eighteenth (White Stars on Red Field) Corps, Army of the James

Figure 58.   Headquarters Flag of the Eighteenth Corps, Army of the James, 1864 to 1865

Figure 59.   Headquarters Flag of the Department of the Cumberland, 1862 to 1864

Figures 60, 61, & 62. Patterns for the Division Flags, Army of the Cumberland, 1862 to 1863

Figure 63.   Headquarters Flag of the Twentieth Corps, Army of the Cumberland, 1863 to 1865

Figure 64.   Headquarters Flag of the Twenty-First Corps, Army of the Cumberland, 1863 to 1865

Figure 65.   Headquarters Flag of the Fourteenth Corps, Army of the Cumberland, 1863 to 1865

Figure 66.   Headquarters Flag of the Reserve Corps, Army of the Cumberland, 1863

Figures 67, 68, & 69. Headquarters Flags of the Divisions of the Reserve Corps, Army of the Cumberland, 1863

Figure 70.   Headquarters Flag of the Cavalry Corps, Army of the Cumberland, 1863

Figure 71.   Pattern for the Headquarters Flags of the Fourth and Fourteenth Corps, Army of the Cumberland, 1864

Figure 72.   Pattern for the Brigade Flags of the Third Divisions of the Fourth and Fourteenth Corps, Army of the Cumberland, 1864

Figure 73.   Headquarters Flag of the Twentieth Corps, Army of the Cumberland, 1864

Figure 74.   Headquarters Flag of the Cavalry Corps, Army of the Cumberland, 1864

Figure 75.   Headquarters Flag of the Twenty-Third Corps, Army of the Ohio, 1864 to 1865

Figure 76.   Pattern of the Division Headquarters Flags of the Twenty-Third Corps, Army of the Ohio, 1864

Figure 77.   Illustration of a Three-Masted Ship Demonstrating the Placement of the Ensign, Jack, and Commission Pennant

Figure 78.   United States Navy "Boat Flag"

Figure 79.   United States Navy Jack, 1861 to 1863

Figure 80.   United States Navy Commission Pennant

Figure 81.   Commodore's Broad Pennant

Figure 82.   Guard Signal

Figure 83.   Church Pennant

Figure 84.   Revenue Service Flag

Figure 85.   Revenue Service Narrow Pennant

Preface

This book is written to be a companion to *The Flags of the Confederacy: An Illustrated History*. Neither is an exhaustive work. There are many individual unit flags which have patterns not shown in these pages. What I have tried to accomplish in the pages of these books is to give the student and historian a good overview of the general types of banners under which the soldiers and sailors of the Confederate States fought for their independence, and under which their counterparts in the United States armed forces fought for a perpetual Union.

Most of the sources for the material in this book are the manuals used by the United States Army and Navy for the period, plus the various general orders which can be found in *The Official Records of the Union and Confederate Armies in the War of the Rebellion*. I am particularly grateful to Howard M. Madaus, curator of the Cody Firearms Museum at the Buffalo Bill Historical Center, Cody, Wyoming; Fred Prouty, archeologist with the Tennessee Department of Environment and Conservation; and Whitney Smith, Ph.D., of the Flag Research Center, Winchester, Massachusetts, for the assistance which they kindly rendered in the preparation of this book.

Introduction

The period 1861 to 1865 was the most devastating time endured by the American people in their history. Citizens who for eighty years and more had worked to forge a common destiny found themselves in arms, fighting the most desperate war in which Americans had ever engaged, and fighting that war against one another.

The soldiers of each army fought for what they believed were the essential principles of American liberty: the Southerner for independence and self-determination; the Northerner for a perpetual Union and the empire of America's "Manifest Destiny." American soldiers have never fought harder than during that time. It is estimated that one out of every four white Southern men was killed in their war for independence, and more Americans died in those four years than in all of America's other wars combined.

The American people have for many years held a deep emotional bond with their flag. Some historians have noted that, when Americans gave up reverence for the trappings of monarchy, they transferred those feelings to an almost religious affection for the flag. That affection can be seen in 1861, when the new Confederate States of America struggled for a month to design a flag, and adopted one dangerously similar to the "Stars and Stripes," and when, after the surrender of Fort Sumter, the North was whipped into a war frenzy by slogans decrying "The Insult to the Flag."

In *The Flags of the Confederacy: An Illustrated History* we examined the banners under which the Southern states fought to establish their independence. In this volume we will examine the flags which guided the Northern armies in the campaign to maintain the Union and build the American empire. Our study will begin with an examination of the development of the most well-known standard, the "Stars and Stripes." We will then proceed to study how that flag and others were utilized by the land and naval forces of the United States during the War Between the States.

THE FLAGS OF THE UNION
AN ILLUSTRATED HISTORY

1
The Stars and Stripes

For the first eleven months of their self-proclaimed independence, the thirteen United States of America had no officially approved common flag. The Bedford Militia had fought at Lexington on April 19, 1775, under a flag which may have been over one hundred years old at the time the "shot heard 'round the world" was fired. Throughout the colonies, rebel armies were fighting under a variety of standards, but the Continental Congress provided no single flag to represent a united America.

At Cambridge, Massachusetts, Gen. George Washington of Virginia assumed command of the American forces. That gathering of citizens could hardly be called an army; but Washington set himself vigorously to the task at hand. As a result, on January 1, 1776, the Continental Army was formally established.

In celebration of the birth of the American army along with the birth of a new year, a seventy-six-foot flagpole was erected on Prospect Hill in Somerville, Massachusetts. It was so high, placed upon the hill, that it could be seen by the British forces in Boston. On that pole on that new year's day was raised what became, in fact if not in law, the first flag of a new nation.

Figure 1: The British Red Ensign

The "Grand Union Flag," as it came to be called, was in appearance a very British symbol; so much so that some British officers in Boston who viewed its debut thought it to be a sign of capitulation by the rebels. The design of the new American flag was based upon the red ensign of the British navy and merchant marine. The American flag preserved the British union of the ensign, but defaced its red field with white stripes, creating thirteen red and white stripes representing the colonies which had united in the rebellion against the royal government.

Figure 2: The Grand Union Flag

The new American flag would soon be seen flying over American fortifications and upon American ships of war. When the American colonies opted for independence in July 1776, this flag became, in effect, the new national flag of the infant United States of America.

It was not until almost a year later, June 14, 1777, that the Continental Congress decided that it was inconsistent for American states attempting to exert their independence from Great Britain to continue to use as their standard a flag which was essentially British. A new flag was adopted by making a minor change in the old one. The British crosses were removed from the blue union and replaced with American stars. The resolution adopted by the Congress read:

Figure 3: The Stars and Stripes

FLAGS OF THE UNION

Resolved: that the flag of the thirteen United States be made of 13 stripes, alternate red and white: that the union be 13 stars, white in a blue field, representing a new constellation.

The resolution adopting a new flag received no immediate attention. The first public notice of it seems to have been in a Philadelphia newspaper reporting on various proceedings of the Congress, on September 2, 1777, almost three months after the resolution was adopted. The "new constellation" saw little use at sea before 1778, and very little use on land until a much later date. General Washington apparently considered it only a naval ensign, referring to it in 1779 as "the Marine Flag," and it was apparently rarely, if ever, used by the regiments of the Continental Army.

The resolution of June 14, 1777, gave almost no particulars on the details of the flag's design. No specifications were set out for the arrangement of the stars, the number of points for the stars, the arrangement and order of colors for the stripes, or the proportions of the blue union. Surviving flags and illustrations of the period indicate that six-, seven-, and eight-pointed stars were more common than five. Although some flags displayed stars arranged in a circle, various arrangements of rows seem to have been more common. Some had the outer stripes red, while others placed the white stripes outermost, and some even included blue stripes. There also seems to have existed a common practice for American merchant ships to fly ensigns that omitted the union and stars altogether, displaying only "the American stripes."

Figure 4: The "American Stripes"

In 1781 the Articles of Confederation were finally ratified by all thirteen states, and the United States began to function formally under their first constitution. In 1783 a peace treaty was signed in which Great Britain recognized her former colonies as free and independent states. Soon, people in places with names such as Vermont and Franklin began to organize state governments and petition for admission to the Confederation Congress, and the American union began to suffer its first growing pains.

In 1787 a convention drafted a proposal for a new form of government. By the end of 1788 this new constitution was ratified by eleven states effectively seceding from the Confederation to create a new United States of America, which began to operate in 1789. By the end of 1790 North Carolina and Rhode Island joined the new union, and the United States were once again thirteen.

One of the changes in the new constitution was the establishment of procedures for the admission of new states into the Union. The first people to benefit from this new provision were the citizens of Vermont. The land of Vermont was claimed by Massachusetts, New Hampshire, and New York. During the Revolution, Vermonters fought to secure their independence not only from Great Britain, but also from their neighboring states. In 1781 Massachusetts assented to Vermont's independence, followed by New Hampshire in 1782. New York finally recognized the Vermont government in 1790 and the following year that state was admitted as the fourteenth state of the American Union.

A fifteenth state would soon follow. At the end of 1789 Virginia adopted an act allowing Kentucky to assume independence and statehood. Kentuckians petitioned Congress for admission, and on February 4, 1791, Congress adopted an act admitting Kentucky to the Union effective the first day of June 1792.

The citizens of the new states wanted to be represented on the flag of the United States. In December 1793, Sen. Steven R. Bradley of Vermont introduced a bill to alter the flag of the United States. The bill was enacted on January 13, 1794, and provided that, effective May 1, 1795, the flag of the United States would be "fifteen stripes, alternate red and white," with the union containing "fifteen stars, white in a blue field."

Figure 5: Flag of the United States, 1795 to 1818

FLAGS OF THE UNION

One year and one month after the new fifteen-star and fifteen-stripe flag became official, Tennessee was admitted to the Union as the sixteenth state. She was followed by Ohio in 1803, Louisiana in 1812, and Indiana in 1816. The flag laws did not change with the admission of these states, the stars and stripes officially remaining at fifteen.

Figure 6: Flag Flown at the U.S. Capitol in 1817

Practice, however, did not necessarily follow the law. While the flag that flew over Fort McHenry in 1814 displayed the legally proper fifteen stars and stripes, the flag atop the federal capitol in 1817 was composed of eighteen stars and stripes. Sporadic debates on again altering the flag were held in Congress in 1816 and 1817, with some preferring to return to the original thirteen stars and stripes, while others suggested thirteen stripes but one star for each state. The latter recommendation was enacted into law on April 4, 1818, as follows:

AN ACT TO ESTABLISH THE FLAG OF THE UNITED STATES

Sect. 1. *Be it enacted by the senate and house of representatives of the United States in congress assembled,* That from and after the fourth day of July next, the flag of the United States be thirteen horizontal stripes, alternate red and white; that the union have twenty stars, white in a blue field.

Sect. 2. *And be it further enacted,* That on the admission of every new State into the Union, one star be added to the union of the flag; and that such addition shall take effect on the fourth day of July next succeeding such admission.

This act set the pattern for the flag to the present day, although there were still no regulations regarding the pattern for the placement of the stars. Throughout the nineteenth century, stars tended to be arranged on the flag in such manner as pleased the manufacturer.

Figure 7: Flag of the United States, 1818 to 1819

From 1818 to 1859 the stars on the United States flag increased from twenty to thirty-three. The members of the Union had grown from the original thirteen on the Atlantic coast until, on July 4, 1859, Oregon on the Pacific coast added its star to the American constellation. Soon, however, that constellation was to be torn asunder.

As the Union grew and prospered, the interests of the Northern and Southern states became more disparate. The South remained predominantly agricultural, while the Industrial Revolution had begun to change the North into a nation of factory workers and merchants. The economic interests of the two sections grew more antagonistic as the years passed, and their representatives in Congress engaged in increasingly bitter debates over such issues as internal improvements, tariffs, and slavery.

The sectional differences climaxed in the presidential election of 1860. The Northern and Southern factions of the Democratic Party split over the issue of "popular sovereignty," the concept that the people of a territory could vote to permit or prohibit slavery in a territory before it became a state. The Northern faction nominated Illinois senator Steven A. Douglas for president, while the Southern Democrats nominated Vice President John C. Breckinridge of Kentucky. The remnants of the Whig Party joined with the American or "Know Nothing" Party to offer Tennessee senator John Bell as the nominee of the Constitutional Union Party. Into this confusion entered the new Republican Party, offering as its candidate a former anti-war (i.e., Mexican War) Congressman from Illinois, Abraham Lincoln.

The Republican platform was strictly geared to the sectional interests of the North, but the fracturing of the Democrats virtually guaranteed Lincoln's election. Although the Republican candidate received less than forty percent of the popular vote, the three-way split among his opposition allowed him to garner a majority of the electoral votes, and victory.

After Lincoln's election, the people of the Deep South felt that the Union no longer guaranteed the constitution's promise of "domestic tranquillity." As a result, on December 20, 1860, a convention of the people of South Carolina adopted an ordinance repealing that state's ratification of the Constitution of the United States of America, and declaring that

> the union . . . between South Carolina and other States, under the name of the "United States of America," is hereby dissolved.

South Carolina was followed in January by Mississippi, Florida, Alabama, Georgia, and Louisiana, and on February 4, 1861, delegates from those six states met in convention in Montgomery, Alabama, to form a new federal government to become known as the Confederate States of America.

Figure 8: Flag of the United States, 1861 to 1863

In the meantime, the United States Congress admitted Kansas to the Union on January 19, 1861. On July 4, 1861, when Kansas' star was officially added to the flag of the United States, the government of the United States was waging war against eleven states which had elected to remove their stars from its flag. Refusing to acknowledge the right of secession, however, the United States government removed no stars from its flag, and Kansas' star became number thirty-four.

Early in the war, some members of the Virginia legislature from that commonwealth's western counties held a rump session, declaring themselves the lawful government of Virginia, and were recognized as such by Lincoln's government. In 1862 this rump legislature voted to allow Virginia's western counties (a number of which were of Confederate sentiment) to be erected into a separate state. Realizing the precarious nature of this action, Lincoln asked his cabinet for their advice. The Attorney General of the United States argued against the admission of West Virginia, pointing out that the body acting as a "loyal" Virginia legislature was obviously without constitutional foundation, and that to dismember Virginia in that way would be to make a mockery of the constitution. Lincoln, however, saw political advantages to West Virginia's electoral votes being available in the 1864 election, and a thirty-fifth star was added to the flag on July 4, 1863.

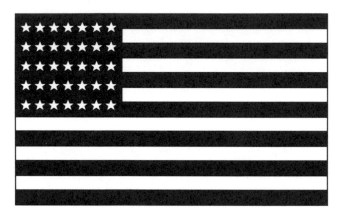

Figure 9: Flag of the United States, 1863 to 1865

The last state to be admitted to the United States during the war was Nevada. She was not admitted until October 31, 1864, however, and her star would not become an official part of the "Stars and Stripes" until July 4, 1865, after the cessation of hostilities. On that date, Gen. Joseph O. Shelby of Missouri lead one of the last organized bodies of Confederate soldiers across the Rio Grande into exile in Mexico.

2

The National Flag
in the United States Army

The flag of the United States served a number of functions in the United States Army during the years of the war against the Confederate States. Some of those functions were and are commonly expected, while others developed for the first time during that period. This chapter will examine the uses of the national flag of the American union at military installations.

I
Garrison Flag

A garrison is a relatively permanent installation for the housing of troops, whether it be a fortress or a training camp. One of the accoutrements of a garrison is a fixed, permanent flagstaff from which is flown the national flag, termed by the military in this case the "garrison flag."

Figure 10: United States Army Garrison Flag,
1861 to 1863

While the United States flag law did not provide specific guidelines for the proportions of the flag or its elements, these oversights were largely remedied in the *Revised Regulations of the Army of the United States*. The garrison flag measured twenty feet in width and thirty-six feet in length. U.S. Army Regulations specified that the blue union of the flag was to extend down to the lower edge of the fourth red stripe and extend out one-third the length of the flag; resulting in the union of the garrison flag measuring over ten feet eight inches in width and twelve feet in length. Each stripe was over one and one-half feet wide. Like the flag law, Army Regulations did not specify how the stars were to be arranged.

II
Storm Flag

The large size of the garrison flag made it and the flagpole susceptible to damage in strong winds. To preserve the flag for economic and aesthetic reasons, a smaller flag called the "storm flag" was flown in the place of the garrison flag in harsh or inclement weather.

Figure 11: United States Army Storm Flag,
1863 to 1865

Regulations specified a length of twenty feet and a width of ten feet for the storm flag. The union was again to be one-third the length of the flag, or six feet eight inches long.

III
Recruiting Flag

Army Regulations established a third size for the national flag specifically to be flown at army recruiting stations. This flag was to be four feet four inches wide and nine feet nine inches long. As with the garrison flag and storm flag, the length of the blue union was to be one-third the length of the flag.

Figure 12: United States Army Recruiting Flag,
1861 to 1863

It is interesting to note that, for the United States flags designed to be flown from fixed poles, the smaller the flag the greater was the length-to-width ratio. The garrison flag's length was 1.8 times its width, the storm flag was twice as long as it was wide, and the recruiting flag's length was two and one-quarter times greater than its breadth. As we shall see, this was not the case with flags designed to be carried into battle.

3
Infantry Colors

The basic unit of the infantry in the nineteenth century was the regiment. A regiment was normally composed of ten companies containing approximately one hundred men each when at full strength. The regiment was commanded by an officer with the rank of colonel, and each company was commanded by a captain.

Each regiment of infantry in the United States Army was to have two flags, called colors. These were made of silk and measured six feet in width and six feet six inches in length. The colors were attached by means of a sleeve to a pike measuring nine feet ten inches in length, including the spear point. Each of the colors was to have a yellow fringe and cords and tassels made of intermixed blue and white silk.

I
The National Color

The first color was the National Color, based on the "Stars and Stripes." As in the case of the garrison flag, the union of the National Color of an infantry regiment was one-third the length of the flag. Since the color was almost square, this resulted in the union of the color being wider on the staff than it was long. The color was made of separately sewn stripes of red and white silk, with a union of blue silk. The stars, usually gold, were painted onto the union.

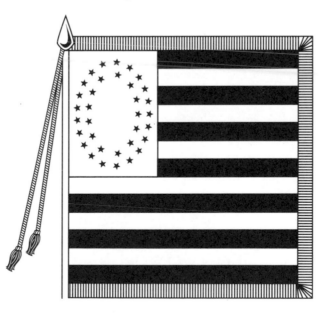

Figure 13: National Color of a U.S. Army Infantry Regiment

According to Army Regulations, the number and name of the regiment were inscribed in silver embroidery on the center stripe. Silver tended to tarnish and turn black, so in practice the regimental designation was most often painted in gold letters.

In February 1862 the United States War Department issued an order stating that

> there shall be inscribed upon the colors or guidons of all regiments and batteries in the service of the United States the names of the battles in which they have borne a meritorious part. These names will also be placed on the Army Register at the head of the list of the officers of each regiment.

Those battle honors were painted on other stripes of the flag. In promulgating the order, the Adjutant-General stated that he

> expected that troops so distinguished will regard their colors as representing the honor of their corps—to be lost only with their lives—and that those not yet entitled to such distinction will not rest satisfied until they have won it by their discipline and courage.

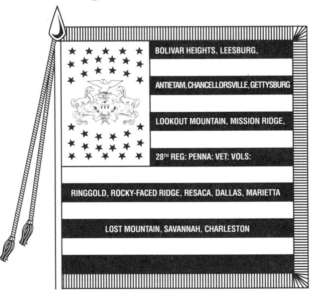

Figure 14: National Color of a Pennsylvania Infantry
Regiment with Battle Honors

The union of the color depicted in Figure 14 is illustrated with the arms of the Commonwealth of Pennsylvania. Many state regiments in the service of the United States carried colors that varied in some details from the specifications of the *Revised Regulations of the Army of the United States*. The Commonwealth of Pennsylvania supplied all volunteer regiments raised by it with a specially made set of "State Colors," such as this, which were used instead of the National Colors.

II
The Regimental Color

The second color carried by United States infantry regiments was the Regimental Color, which was a blue silk flag, the same size as the National Color. The blue field was decorated with the "arms of the United States": the eagle with federal shield, olive branch and arrows, arched over with stars, all embroidered or painted on the silk. The name and number of the regiment were painted on a red scroll below the eagle.

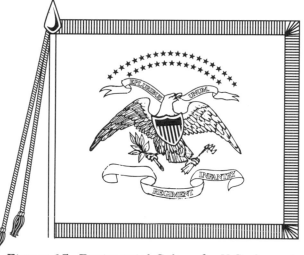

Figure 15: Regimental Color of a U.S. Army Infantry
Regiment

The Regimental Color had originally been used in the army as the National Color. Prior to 1841 infantry regiments of the United States did not march or fight under the "Stars and Stripes." The blue flag with the "arms of the United States" served as the National Color, while a white flag (yellow before 1834) with

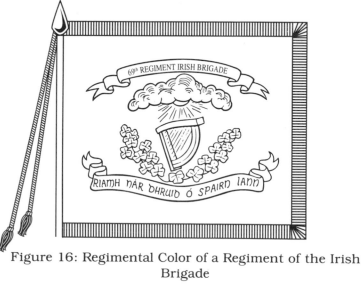

Figure 16: Regimental Color of a Regiment of the Irish
Brigade

Infantry Colors

the regimental designation on a scroll served as the Regimental Color. The war with Mexico in 1846 was the first war in which United States infantry regiments were authorized to carry the "Stars and Stripes."

During the War Between the States many of the volunteer regiments raised were presented Regimental Colors bearing designs differing from that prescribed by Army Regulations. These often had some special significance to the particular regiment. Perhaps the most famous of these are the various green flags presented to Irish units.

When an infantry regiment was formed for battle, it would be lined up in two ranks, with the men shoulder to shoulder. A solid line of ten companies, at full strength, would total about one thousand men. The captains and first sergeants were posted on the right of their respective companies, the captain on the front rank and the first sergeant directly behind him in the rear rank.

The lieutenants and other sergeants were posted behind each company in a third line called the "file closers." Their job was to maintain the company's alignment and to repeat the captain's orders so that all could hear their instructions.

The company immediately to the right of the center of the regiment was designated as the "color company." Immediately to the color company's left, in the exact center of the regiment, was placed the color guard.

The National and Regimental Colors were carried by sergeants designated by the colonel of the regiment to be "color bearers." The color sergeants were to "be selected from those most distinguished for regularity and precision in marching, and a just carriage of the person." The color guard was composed of the color sergeants and eight to ten corporals. The latter were chosen "from the most distinguished as well in their distinction under arms as in marching." The color sergeants, flanked by two corporals, were placed in the front rank of the regiment. Four corporals were placed behind in the rear rank, and the remaining members of the color guard were placed on the line of the file closers.

The importance of the color guard can be seen in the requirements set for its composition. When the regiment moved forward in a line of battle, the pace for the movement was set by the color guard. One thousand men would "guide on the colors." Regularity and precision of movement by the color guard were necessary for regularity and precision of movement by the regiment. It was for that reason that such strict requirements were set for membership in the color guard—and it was for that same reason that the colors were so heavily guarded and so often the target of heavy enemy fire. To take or shoot down an enemy regiment's colors was to destroy the principal means of directing its movements in battle. To do so would impair the effectiveness and morale of that regiment. Rare indeed was the color guard that emerged unscathed from heavy combat.

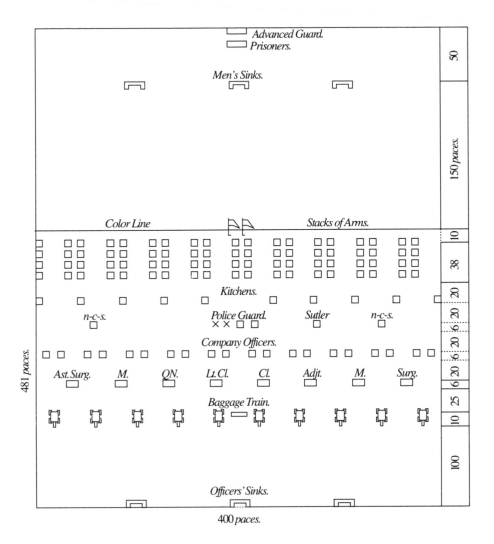

Figure 17: Diagram of the Camp of an Infantry
Regiment

When an infantry regiment went into camp, it would form in line of battle at a predetermined spot designated the "color line." The colors were planted at the center of the color line, and the troops tacked their muskets in a line extending from either side of the colors, along the color line. The regimental encampment was then formed behind the color line, each company establishing a company street running back from the color line between two rows of tents.

III
Camp Colors

Figure 18: Camp Colors Authorized Prior to 1862

Each regiment was also provided with a number of flags called "camp colors." The camp colors were made of bunting, eighteen inches square, and mounted on a pole eight feet long. Prior to 1862 the camp colors for infantry regiments were white with the number of the regiment centered on them.

On January 7, 1862, the United States Secretary of War issued instructions stating that thenceforth the camp colors would "be made like the United States flag, with stars and stripes." Although the new regulations did not specifically change the dimensions of the camp colors, those printed in the "Stars and Stripes" pattern tended to be eighteen inches wide by about twenty inches long.

Figure 19: Camp Colors after January 1862

Camp colors were used to mark off the regiment's camp and the color line. They were also used for some parade maneuvers. For example, in preparing for the review of an infantry regiment, the regimental adjutant would cause a camp color to the placed eighty to one hundred paces "in front of, and opposite to, where the centre of the [regiment] would rest." The reviewing officer would usually take up his position beside the camp color; but even if he quit that position, all movements and formations of the regiment would be made relative to the posting of the camp color.

IV
Flank and General Guide Markers

Many infantry regiments used flank markers or general guide markers. These were small flags carried by sergeants posted at each end of a regiment in line of battle. The flank markers were to mark the extreme ends of a straight line, with the National and Regimental Colors marking the center of the line, along which the entire regiment was to form.

Army Regulations did not call for these markers, but tradition (and their usefulness in perfecting alignment) seems to have demanded them. Often camp colors would be used to serve the function of flank markers. At times cavalry guidons (see Chapter 4) were pressed into service by infantry units for this purpose.

The difference between flank markers and general guide markers was merely in the means of display. Like the camp colors, flank markers were attached to an eight-foot pole. General guide markers were mounted on a small staff designed to fit into the bore of the sergeant's musket.

4
Standards and Guidons
of Cavalry Regiments

I
The Standard

The cavalry had its own nomenclature distinct from that of the infantry. What was called a "color" in the infantry was termed a "standard" when used in the cavalry. While the infantry's National Color had used the design of the "Stars and Stripes" since 1841, when the United States Cavalry rode off to war in 1861 no mounted unit was authorized to carry the flag of the United States in any form.

Figure 20: Standard of a U.S. Cavalry Regiment

The cavalry standard was a small version of the infantry Regimental Color. Since cavalry regiments only used one standard, the cavalry's use of the blue National Standard was not changed in 1841. Like the infantry's Regimental Color, the cavalry standard was a blue silk flag embroidered with the arms of the United States. The regimental designation appeared on a scroll beneath the eagle. The standard was much smaller than the infantry color, measuring two feet three inches on the lance by two feet five inches in length.

In some cases, state cavalry regiments were presented special standards. In most cases these were unique flags, not of a pattern. The Commonwealth of Pennsylvania, however, issued state standards to her cavalry regiments. The Pennsylvania standard corresponded to those called for by federal regulations, except that the federal eagle was replaced with the arms of the commonwealth.

Figure 21: Regimental Standard of a Pennsylvania
Cavalry Regiment

II
Guidons

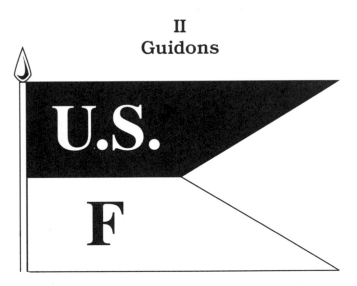

Figure 22: U.S. Cavalry Guidon Prior to 1862

    Each company or troop of cavalry carried a guidon. The guidon measured two feet three inches on the lance, the same width as the regimental standard. The length of the guidon was three feet five inches from the lance to the end of the swallow-tail, and fifteen inches from the lance to the fork of the swallow-tail.

    The old-style guidon, still used in 1861, was divided horizontally, red over white. On the red appeared the letters "U.S." in white. The company letter was placed in red on the lower white portion.

Figure 23: U.S. Cavalry Guidon after January 1862

In 1862 the "Stars and Stripes" finally joined the U.S. Cavalry. The same directive from the War Department that made the national flag the pattern for infantry camp colors (Chapter 3), also provided that cavalry guidons "will be made like the United States flag, with stars and stripes."

Regulations specified that the lances for both the regimental standard and the guidons were to be nine feet long, including the spear point.

5
Colors of Artillery Regiments

The Corps of Artillery was the first branch of the United States Army to be authorized to use the flag of the United States as a National Color. That authority was given in 1834, seven years before it was granted to the infantry and twenty-eight years before the cavalry was authorized to use the "Stars and Stripes" as a guidon.

The regulations for the artillery's National Color were nearly identical to those for the infantry, described in Chapter 3. A major difference was that the cords and tassels were to be of red and yellow silk intermixed. Also, the unit designation for the artillery was to be embroidered in gold on the center stripe.

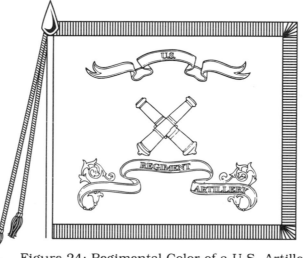

Figure 24: Regimental Color of a U.S. Artillery
Regiment

The Regimental Color for the artillery service was to be made of yellow silk. Like the Regimental Color for infantry, it was to be six feet wide, six feet six inches in length, and edged with a yellow fringe. In the center of the color were two bronze cannon, crossed. On a scroll above the cannon were the gold letters "U.S." The regimental designation was displayed on another scroll below the cannon.

As a rule, the active component of the artillery was the battery. In 1861 each artillery regiment was composed of ten to twelve batteries, but in 1863 the number was reduced to six. Each battery was armed with four to six cannon. Rarely did the batteries serve together as a regiment. In most cases, the colors remained at regimental headquarters, which served as little more than an administrative center. In some cases, heavy artillery regiments would be armed and fight as infantry. In those instances the National and Regimental Colors of the artillery regiment were carried into combat in the same manner as infantry colors.

Although the regulations were silent on the matter, individual artillery batteries were supplied with guidons. Those guidons were usually of the same pattern as those described for the cavalry in Chapter 4.

6
The Medical Service

Military hospitals and ambulances flew flags to show their function. These distinctive flags helped those in need of their services to find them, and served to protect them from hostile fire, to which they were supposed to be immune.

Originally a plain yellow flag was used. (See the discussion of the flag of the Army of the Cumberland in Chapter 7.) This was derived from the use of a yellow flag by the navy as a quarantine flag. On January 4, 1864, the U.S. War Department issued General Order No. 9, establishing a formal system of flags and guidons for the medical service.

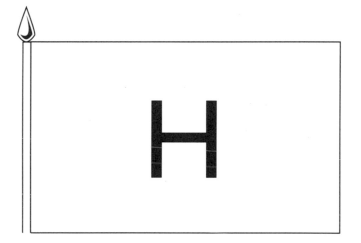

Figure 25: U.S. Army Hospital Flag

The flag flown by general hospitals was yellow bunting, five feet wide and nine feet long. In the center of the flag was a letter "H" made of green bunting, twenty-four inches high.

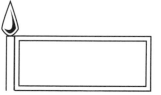

Figure 26: U.S. Medical Service Guidon

The flag used by field hospitals was of the same design. It measured four feet by six feet. The letter "H" on this smaller flag was the same size as on the general hospital flag.

General Order No. 9 also prescribed a guidon to be made of yellow bunting. The guidon was fourteen inches wide and twenty-eight inches long, with a one-inch green border. It was attached to ambulances and was used to mark the way to field hospitals.

7
Designating Flags

Throughout the war a variety of flags were designed for use to designate the headquarters of the armies, and their corps, divisions, and brigades. Army commanders found these designating flags helpful in keeping track of where all of their various subordinate commanders and their commands were located during the course of a campaign.

In Chapter 3 we examined the composition of an infantry regiment. At this point we shall learn some definitions for the terms used to designate the larger units of the military service.

BRIGADE: A unit composed of several regiments, supposed to be commanded by a brigadier general (one star), but often commanded by a colonel.

DIVISION: A unit composed of two or more brigades, supposed to be commanded by a major general (two stars).

CORPS: A unit composed of three or four divisions, supposed to be commanded by a lieutenant general (three stars).

ARMY: A unit composed of two or more corps, supposed to be commanded by a full general (four stars), but usually commanded during the war by a lieutenant general.

DEPARTMENT: A military command covering a specified geographic area, often, but not necessarily, corresponding to the operational area of an army.

The headquarters of generals commanding armies were usually designated by the flag of the United States, often about the size of the recruiting flag described in Chapter 2. Sometimes those flags had some extra device added to

Figure 27: General Grant's Headquarters Flag, 1864
to 1865

the union, such as an eagle or a shield. More often, the designating flag for the army commander would be a plain federal flag, such as that used by Gen. Ulysses S. Grant during the last year of the war.

A notable exception to the rule was the headquarters flag adopted for the Army of the Potomac by Gen. George G. Meade on May 2, 1864. That flag was a "magenta-colored swallow-tailed flag, with an eagle in gold, surrounded by a silver wreath for an emblem." The war artist A. R. Waud recorded that, when General Grant first saw this flag, he exclaimed, "What's this! Is Imperial Caesar anywhere about here?"

Figure 28: Headquarters Flag of the Army of the
Potomac, 1864 to 1865

Let us now examine some of the designating flags used in the United States Army. Our study will take us first to the Eastern Theater, after which we will look to the West.

I
Army of the Potomac

The Army of the Potomac was the largest of the U.S. armies. It had the primary objective of waging war in Virginia and attempting the capture of the Confederate States' capitol at Richmond. During the course of the war it contained a total of eleven corps.

The designating flags used by the corps of the Army of the Potomac were blue swallow-tails. They measured three feet wide and were six feet long from the pike to the tip of the swallow-tail. Each flag was marked with a distinctive insignia and usually displayed the corps number.

The headquarters of the several divisions within each corps were marked by a white or blue oblong flag. These measured four and one-half feet wide by six feet in length. The corps badge was displayed in the center of the division flag.

First Corps

The emblem on the blue swallow-tail headquarters flag of the First Corps was a white "Tunic cross" with the numeral "1" in red in the center.

Figure 29: Headquarters Flag of the First Corps, Army
of the Potomac, 1863 to 1865

The corps badge of the First Corps was a disc. That badge was reproduced on the headquarters flags of each of the divisions of that corps. The flag of the First Division displayed a red disc on a white field. The Second Division's flag was a white disc on a blue field, while that of the Third Division was a blue disc on a white field.

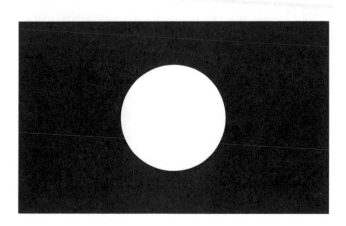

Figure 30: Pattern of Division Headquarters Flags,
First Corps, Army of the Potomac

Second Corps

The headquarters flag of the Second Corps was adorned with the corps badge. Called a "trefoil," it resembled a shamrock. The trefoil was white with the red numeral "2" in the center.

Figure 31: Headquarters Flag of the Second Corps,
Army of the Potomac, 1864 to 1865

The corps badge was repeated on the designating flags for the division headquarters. The color combinations used duplicated those of the divisions of the First Corps. Those combinations were used for the divisions of most of the Army of the Potomac's corps; that is, a red device on white for the First Division, white on blue for the Second Division, and blue and white for the Third Division.

Figure 32: Pattern of Division Headquarters Flags,
Second Corps, Army of the Potomac

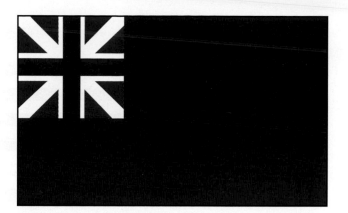

Figure 1: The British Red Ensign

Figure 2: The Grand Union Flag

Figure 3: The Stars and Stripes

Figure 4: The "American Stripes" (Unofficial Merchant Ensign of
the Late 18th and Early 19th Centuries)

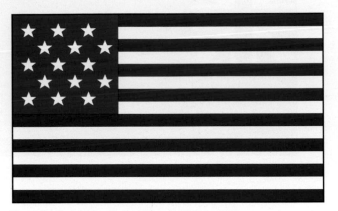
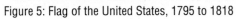

Figure 5: Flag of the United States, 1795 to 1818

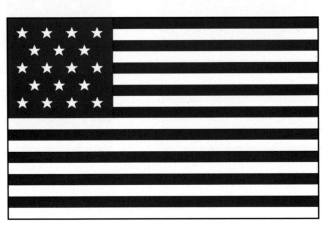

Figure 6: Flag Flown at the U.S. Capitol in 1817

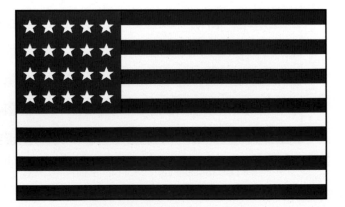

Figure 7: Flag of the United States, 1818 to 1819

Figure 8: Flag of the United States, 1861 to 1863

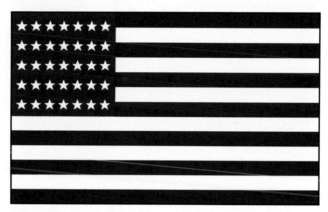

Figure 9: Flag of the United States, 1863 to 1865

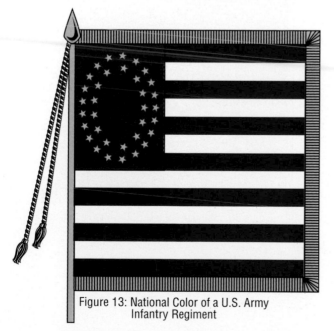

Figure 13: National Color of a U.S. Army
Infantry Regiment

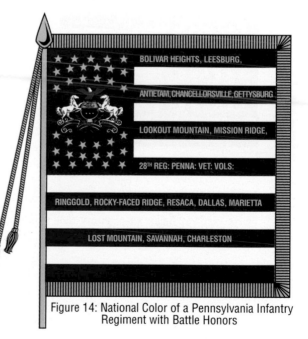

Figure 14: National Color of a Pennsylvania Infantry
Regiment with Battle Honors

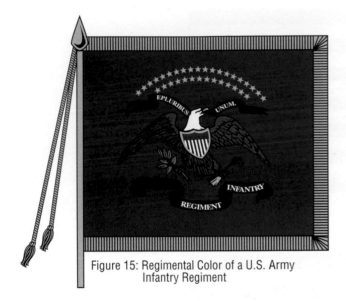

Figure 15: Regimental Color of a U.S. Army
Infantry Regiment

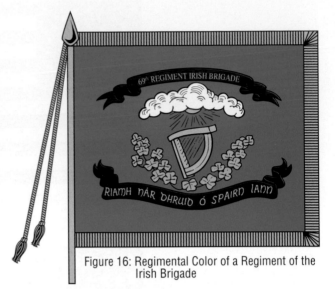

Figure 16: Regimental Color of a Regiment of the
Irish Brigade

Figure 19: Camp Colors after January 1862

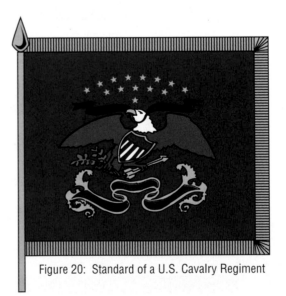

Figure 20: Standard of a U.S. Cavalry Regiment

Figure 21: Regimental Standard of a Pennsylvania
Cavalry Regiment

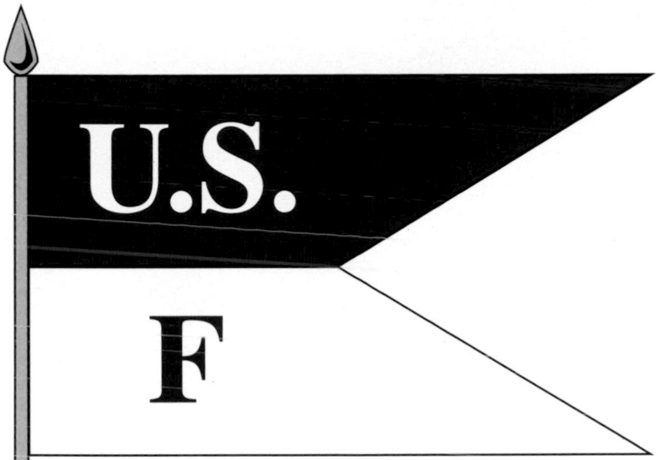

Figure 22: U.S. Cavalry Guidon prior to 1862

Figure 23: U.S. Cavalry Guidon after January 1862

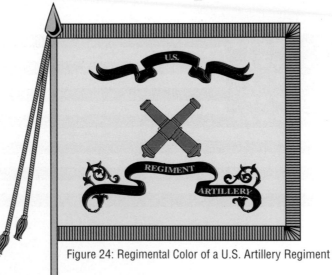

Figure 24: Regimental Color of a U.S. Artillery Regiment

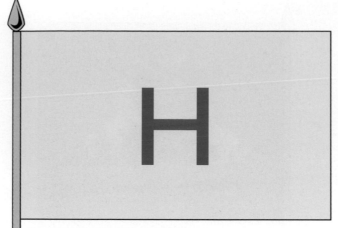

Figure 25: U.S. Army Hospital Flag

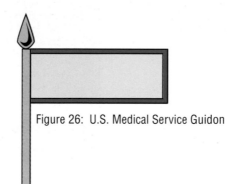

Figure 26: U.S. Medical Service Guidon

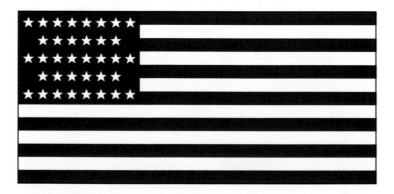

Figure 27: General Grant's Headquarters Flag, 1864 to 1865

Figure 28: Headquarters Flag of the Army of the Potomac,
1864 to 1865

Figure 29: Headquarters Flag of the First Corps, Army of the
Potomac, 1863 to 1865

Figure 31: Headquarters Flag of the Second Corps, Army of the
Potomac, 1864 to 1865

Figure 33: Headquarters Flag of the Third Corps, Army of the Potomac, 1864 to 1865

Figure 35: Headquarters Flag of the Fifth Corps, Army of the Potomac, 1864 to 1865

Figure 37: Headquarters Flag of the Sixth Corps, Army of the Potomac, 1864 to 1865

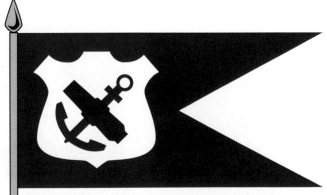

Figure 39: Headquarters Flag of the Ninth Corps, Army of the Potomac, 1864 to 1865

Figure 41: Headquarters Flag of the Eleventh Corps, Army of the Potomac, 1864 to 1865

Figure 43: Headquarters Flag of the Twelfth Corps, Army of the Potomac, 1864 to 1865

Figure 45: Headquarters Flag of the Nineteenth Corps, Army of the Potomac, 1864 to 1865

Figure 47: Headquarters Flag of the Twenty-Fourth Corps, Army of the Potomac, 1864 to 1865

Figure 49: Headquarters Flag of the Twenty-Fifth Corps, Army of the Potomac, 1864 to 1865

Figure 51: Headquarters Flag of the Cavalry Corps, Army of the Potomac, 1864 to 1865

Figure 53: Headquarters Flag of the Department of Virginia and North Carolina, 1864 to 1865

Figure 54: Headquarters Flag of the Tenth Corps,
Army of the James, 1864 to 1865

Figure 58: Headquarters Flag of the Eighteenth
Corps, Army of the James, 1864 to 1865

Figure 59: Headquarters Flag of the Department of the
Cumberland, 1862 to 1864

Figure 63: Headquarters Flag of the
Twentieth Corps,
Army of the Cumberland,
1863 to 1865

Figure 64: Headquarters Flag of the
Twenty-First Corps,
Army of the Cumberland,
1863 to 1865

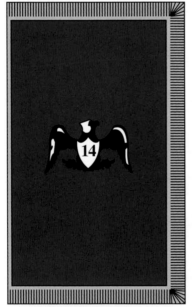

Figure 65: Headquarters Flag of the
Fourteenth Corps,
Army of the Cumberland,
1863 to 1865

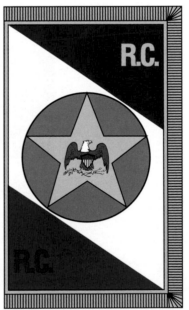

Figure 66: Headquarters Flag of the
Reserve Corps, Army of the
Cumberland, 1863

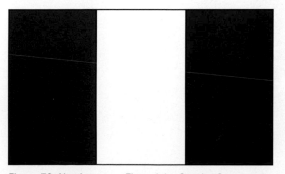

Figure 67: Headquarters Flag of the First Division of the Reserve Corps, Army of the Cumberland, 1863

Figure 68: Headquarters Flag of the Second Division of the Reserve Corps, Army of the Cumberland, 1863

Figure 69: Headquarters Flag of the Third Division of the Reserve Corps, Army of the Cumberland, 1863

Figure 70: Headquarters Flag of the Cavalry Corps, Army of the Cumberland, 1863

Figure 73: Headquarters Flag of the Twentieth Corps, Army of the Cumberland, 1864

Figure 74: Headquarters Flag of the Cavalry Corps,
Army of the Cumberland, 1864

Figure 75: Headquarters Flag of the
Twenty-Third Corps,
Army of the Ohio,
1864 to 1865

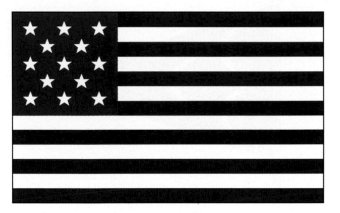

Figure 78: United States Navy "Boat Flag"

Figure 79: United States Navy Jack, 1861 to 1863

Figure 80: United States Navy Commission Pennant

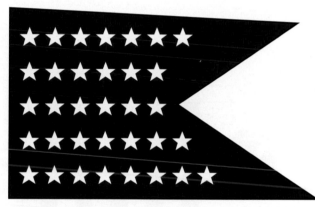

Figure 81: Commodore's Broad Pennant

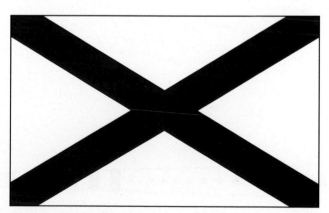

Figure 82: Guard Signal

Figure 83: Church Pennant

Figure 84: Revenue Service Flag

Figure 85: Revenue Service Narrow Pennant

Third Corps

The headquarters flag of the Third Corps was almost identical to that of the First Corps. The only difference was the substitution of the numeral "3" for the "1" in the center of the Tunic cross.

Figure 33: Headquarters Flag of the Third Corps,
Army of the Potomac, 1864 to 1865

The badge of the Third Corps was a diamond. It was displayed on the flags of that corps' division headquarters in the same color combinations as those described for the corps previously discussed.

Figure 34: Pattern of Division Headquarters Flags,
Third Corps, Army of the Potomac

Fifth Corps

The Fourth Corps served in the Western Theater. It will be covered with the other corps of that theater of the war. The badge of the Fifth Corps was a "Maltese cross." It was repeated on the corps and division designation flags in the same manner as on the flags of the Second Corps.

Figure 35: Headquarters Flag of the Fifth Corps, Army of the Potomac, 1864 to 1865

Figure 36: Pattern of Division Headquarters Flags, Fifth Corps, Army of the Potomac

Sixth Corps

Prior to August 1, 1864, the badge of the Sixth Corps had been a Greek cross. On that date it was changed to a saltier, or Saint Andrew's cross. The saltier was represented on the flags of the Sixth Corps in the same pattern as other corps and division flags of the Army of the Potomac.

Figure 37: Headquarters Flag of the Sixth Corps,
Army of the Potomac, 1864 to 1865

Figure 38: Pattern of Division Headquarters Flags,
Sixth Corps, Army of the Potomac

Ninth Corps

The badge of the Ninth Corps was a shield on which were crossed an anchor and a cannon. Prior to his command joining the Army of the Potomac, this device appeared in the union of the federal flag which marked Gen. Ambrose Burnside's headquarters. On the corps headquarters flag the shield was white, with the anchor and cannon blue and red, respectively.

Figure 39: Headquarters Flag of the Ninth Corps,
Army of the Potomac, 1864 to 1865

There were four divisions in the Ninth Corps. The headquarters designating flag of the First Division displayed a red shield with white anchor and blue cannon on a white field. A white shield with blue anchor and red cannon on a blue field identified the Second Division. The Third Division's white flag displayed a blue shield with a red anchor and white cannon, and that of the Fourth Division, also a white flag, had a green shield with white anchor and red cannon.

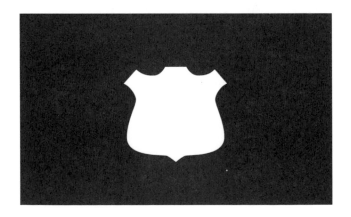

Figure 40: Pattern of Division Headquarters Flags,
Ninth Corps, Army of the Potomac

Eleventh Corps

The headquarters flag of the Eleventh Corps copied the headquarters flags of the First and Third Corps, placing a red "11" in the center of the Tunic cross.

Figure 41: Headquarters Flag of the Eleventh Corps,
Army of the Potomac, 1864 to 1865

A crescent moon, its points directed toward the viewer's left, was the badge of the Eleventh Corps, and was displayed on the division designating flags in the same color combinations as used on the division flags of the First, Second, Third, Fifth, and Sixth Corps; i.e., a red device on white for the First Division, white on blue for the Second Division, and blue and white for the Third Division.

Figure 42: Pattern of Division Headquarters Flags,
Eleventh Corps, Army of the Potomac

Twelfth Corps

The Twelfth Corps used the same Tunic cross headquarters flag used by the First, Third, and Eleventh Corps. The badge of the Twelfth Corps was a star, which was displayed on the division designating flags in the same color patterns as was found on the division flags of the Eleventh Corps, and most other corps of the Army of the Potomac.

Figure 43: Headquarters Flag of the Twelfth Corps,
Army of the Potomac, 1864 to 1865

Figure 44: Pattern of Division Headquarters Flags,
Twelfth Corps, Army of the Potomac

Nineteenth Corps

The badge of the Nineteenth Corps was a variant of the Maltese cross, similar, but not identical, to that used by the Fifth Corps. The corps headquarters designating flag was the usual blue swallow-tail, decorated with the corps badge in white and the corps numerals centered on the badge in red.

Figure 45: Headquarters Flag of the Nineteenth
Corps, Army of the Potomac, 1864 to 1865

Perhaps because of the similarity between the badges of the Fifth and Nineteenth Corps, the division designating flags of the latter did not follow the norm for other corps of the Army of the Potomac. The Nineteenth Corps division headquarters flags were triangular pennants. They measured three feet eight inches in width on the lance, and had a length of five feet six inches. The First Division's flag showed the corps badge in white on a red pennant. The Second Division had a blue cross on a white pennant. The pennant of the Third Division was blue with a white cross.

Figure 46: Pattern of Division Headquarters Flags,
Nineteenth Corps, Army of the Potomac

Twenty-Fourth Corps

The Twenty-Fourth Corps' badge was a heart, which was displayed on its designating flags in the manner common to most corps of the Army of the Potomac.

Figure 47: Headquarters Flag of the Twenty-Fourth Corps, Army of the Potomac, 1864 to 1865

Figure 48: Pattern of Division Headquarters Flags, Twenty-Fourth Corps, Army of the Potomac

Twenty-Fifth Corps

The badge of the Twenty-Fifth Corps was a square. The flags of this corps followed the same color scheme common for the Army of the Potomac, but the sizes and dimensions were different. The designating flag for the corps headquarters measured two feet in width and five feet nine inches from the lance to the points of the swallow-tail. The flags used to mark the division headquarters were two feet seven inches wide and five feet nine inches long.

Figure 49: Headquarters Flag of the Twenty-Fifth Corps, Army of the Potomac, 1864 to 1865

Figure 50: Pattern of Division Headquarters Flags, Twenty-Fifth Corps, Army of the Potomac

Cavalry Corps

The designating flags for the Cavalry Corps of the Army of the Potomac followed the pattern used by most of the infantry corps of that army. The corps headquarters flag was a three-foot-wide by six-foot-long blue swallow-tail with the crossed sabers of the cavalry service in white, superimposed by a red "C." The headquarters designating flags of the cavalry divisions were four feet six inches wide and six feet long. The flag of the First Division displayed red sabers on a white field. The Second Division's flags had white sabers on a blue field, while that of the Third Division showed blue crossed sabers on white.

Figure 51: Headquarters Flag of the Cavalry Corps,
Army of the Potomac, 1864 to 1865

Figure 52: Pattern of Division Headquarters Flags,
Cavalry Corps, Army of the Potomac

II
Army of the James

The Army of the James operated largely in the United States Military Department of Virginia and North Carolina. It often cooperated with the Army of the

Potomac in the campaigns of 1864 and 1865. It was composed of the Tenth and Eighteenth Army Corps.

The designating flag for the headquarters of the Department of Virginia and North Carolina, as described by the commanding general in May 1864, was "6 feet square, two horizontal bars, upper bar red, lower bar blue, with a white star in the center."

Figure 53: Headquarters Flag of the Department of
Virginia and North Carolina, 1864 to 1865

Tenth Corps

The designating flag of the Tenth Corps was blue, six feet square, with the numeral "10" in white. The designating flags for the divisions were of the same color and size, with one, two, and three white stars each, respectively, for the First, Second, and Third Divisions.

Figure 54: Headquarters Flag of the Tenth Corps,
Army of the James, 1864 to 1865

Figure 55: Pattern for Headquarters Flag of the First Division, Tenth (White Star on Blue Field) and Eighteenth (White Star on Red Field) Corps, Army of the James

Figure 56: Pattern for Headquarters Flag of the Second Division, Tenth (White Stars on Blue Field) and Eighteenth (White Stars on Red Field) Corps, Army of the James

Figure 57: Pattern for Headquarters Flag of the Third
Division, Tenth (White Stars on Blue Field) and
Eighteenth (White Stars on Red Field) Corps,
Army of the James

Eighteenth Corps

The General Order of May 3, 1864, established that the headquarters designating flag of the Eighteenth Corps would be a red flag, six feet square, with the white numeral "18" in the center.

Figure 58: Headquarters Flag of the Eighteenth
Corps, Army of the James, 1864 to 1865

The division flags for this corps followed the same pattern as those of the Tenth Corps, but substituting a red field for the blue field used by the Tenth Corps' divisions. These flags replaced division flags which had been promulgated by Major General Foster under General Order No. 13 on January 12, 1863. Those flags were six feet wide and nine feet long. At the time, the Eighteenth Corps contained five divisions. The flags of the First, Third, and Fifth Divisions were divided into two horizontal bars: red over white for the First Division, blue over white for the Third Division, and red over blue for the Fifth Division. The flag of the Second Division was a plain red field, and that of the Fourth Division, an unadorned blue flag.

III
Army of the Cumberland

The area encompassed within the United States Military Department of the Cumberland included East and Middle Tennessee and the northern portions of Alabama and Georgia.

In December 1862 the Army of the Cumberland was made up only of the Fourteenth Army Corps. On December 14, 1862, Maj. Gen. William S. Rosecrans issued General Order No. 41 designating flags for the Department. The Department Headquarters flag was described as "the National flag, 6 feet by 5, with a golden eagle below the stars, 2 feet from tip to tip."

Figure 59: Headquarters Flag of the Department of the Cumberland, 1862 to 1864

FLAGS OF THE UNION

The Fourteenth Corps was, at that time, extraordinarily large. When most army corps were composed of three or four divisions, the Fourteenth Corps had nine. In organizing his army, Rosecrans divided the Fourteenth Corps into three sub-corps which he called "wings," and authorized a distinctive set of designating flags for each. The flags of wing headquarters were to be six feet on the staff by four on the fly. The flag of the Right Wing was a "plain light crimson flag." A similar flag of light blue was designated for the Center Wing, and one of pink for the Left Wing.

Each division of the various corps was to designate its headquarters with a flag of the same color as the flag of the wing to which it was attached. The division flags measured five feet on the staff and three feet in length. The flag of the First Division of each wing was to have a single eighteen-inch diameter star centered on the staff, with the inner point one inch from the staff. Each Second Division flag had two stars equidistant along the staff. The Third Division flags added a third star, forming a triangle with the other two stars, the outer star measuring one inch from the fly edge of the flag.

Figures 60, 61, & 62: Patterns for the Division Flags,
Army of the Cumberland, 1862 to 1863

The headquarters flag of each brigade, except "the brigade of regulars," was to be the flag of the respective division, "with the numeral of the brigade in black, 8 inches long, in the center of each star." The "brigade of regulars," which was the Fourth Brigade of the First Division, Center Wing, commanded by Lt. Col. Oliver L. Shepherd, used as its headquarters flag a light blue flag with an unmarked gold star.

The headquarters flag of the cavalry was to be of the same style and shape as for the infantry divisions, with the same use of stars and brigade numbers, but of a deep orange color. The artillery reserve marked its headquarters with a plain red flag, five feet square. The Engineer Corps' flag was five feet wide by three feet long, divided horizontally, blue over white. Hospitals and the principal ambulance depot were designated by light yellow flags three feet square. Lesser ambulance depots were marked by two-foot-square yellow flags. Subsistence depots and storehouses were marked with three-foot square flags of light green, and quartermaster's depots and storehouses used the same flag marked with the letters "Q.M.D." in white, one foot high.

General Order No. 41 specified that all of the above mentioned flags were to

> be attached to a portable staff, 14 feet long, made in two joints, and will be habitually displayed in front of the tent, or from a prominent part of the house or vessel occupied by the officer, whose headquarters they are intended to designate; and on the march will be carried near his person.

It was determined, apparently during the battle of Murfreesboro (Stones River), that the designating flags of the Department of the Cumberland were "not sufficiently marked to be readily distinguished from each other." As a result, on April 25, 1863, General Rosecrans issued General Order No. 91. This order created a new system of designating flags for the Army of the Cumberland. The new order left unchanged the flags of the department headquarters, the Engineer Corps, hospitals, ambulances, and subsistence and quartermaster's depots and storehouses. All other designating flags changed.

At the time General Order No. 91 was issued, the Army of the Cumberland was divided into three corps rather than "wings." On February 2, 1863, the Fourteenth Corps was divided to create, in addition, the Twentieth and Twenty-First Corps.

The flag of the Twentieth Corps was bright red, measuring six feet on the staff and having a fly length of four feet. It was fringed, "with a black eagle in center, 2 feet from tip to tip," with the numeral "20" in black on a white shield on the eagle's breast.

Figure 63: Headquarters Flag of the Twentieth Corps,
Army of the Cumberland, 1863 to 1865

The Twenty-First Corps used a flag of the same size as that of the Twentieth Corps. The field, however, was divided into colored panels, two feet wide: red at the top, white in the middle, and blue at the bottom. The same eagle as used on the Twentieth Corps' flag was placed on the white panel of the Twenty-First Corps' flag, with the numeral "21" on the shield.

Figure 64: Headquarters Flag of the Twenty-First
Corps, Army of the Cumberland, 1863 to 1865

Designating Flags

The flags of the divisions matched those of the corps in general color patterns. They were not fringed, and rather than being marked with a black eagle, they displayed eighteen-inch black stars, numbering one, two, or three "according as they represent the first, second, third, &c., divisions." If one star, it was placed in the center of the flag's width, and about an inch from the flag staff. When two or three stars were present, they were placed at even intervals on the field, again about one inch from the staff, one over the other. Designating flags for brigades were the same as the flag of the respective division "with the number of the brigade in white, 8 inches long, in the center of each star."

The flag of the Fourteenth Corps was to be "[a] bright blue flag, six feet by 4 feet, fringed, with black eagle in center, two feet from tip to tip, with the number '14' in black on shield, which shall be white." As with the other two corps of the Army of the Cumberland, the division and brigade flags were to match the color of the corps flag with black stars to indicate the number of the division, and the brigade number in the stars on brigade flags. When the division and brigade flags for the Fourteenth Corps were received, however, they were made of dark blue material, rather than the bright blue specified. The black stars were virtually invisible on the dark blue flags. As a result, on August 1, 1863, General Order No. 177 prescribed that the division flags of the Fourteenth Corps would be dark blue with white stars in accordance with the number of the division. Brigade flags were to place black numerals on the white stars.

Figure 65: Headquarters Flag of the Fourteenth
Corps, Army of the Cumberland, 1863 to 1865

FLAGS OF THE UNION

The brigade of regulars, which had its own distinctive flag under the 1862 system, was given the same distinction in 1863. That brigade, now commanded by Brig. Gen. John H. King, was the Third Brigade, First Division, Fourteenth Army Corps. General King's headquarters was marked by a dark blue flag, six feet wide and four feet long, with a gold star centered on and two inches from the staff.

In the summer of 1863 a Reserve Corps was created, and General Order No. 177 also ordered a system of flags for that corps. The Reserve Corps headquarters flag was fringed, the same size as other corps flags. Its colors were red, white, and blue arranged in diagonal bars. The red formed a triangle in the upper right portion of the flag, with the gold letters "R.C." on it. The blue triangle in the lower left of the flag was marked with the same lettering in red. In the center of the white stripe was a circle of light blue "containing a five pointed golden star, partially covered by an eagle perched upon a shield, upon which is emblazoned the stars and stripes."

Figure 66: Headquarters Flag of the Reserve Corps,
Army of the Cumberland, 1863

The division flags of the Reserve Corps were pennants. They were three feet wide and had a length of four and one-half feet to the point of the fly. These pennants were divided horizontally, red over blue. Each division's flag was marked with white crescents corresponding in number to the number of the division. Brigade headquarters were designated by a pennant matching that of their divisions, "with the addition of a figure in white, equidistant from the staff and the crescent, to denote the number of the brigade." Artillery batteries of the Reserve Corps had flags of red, white, and blue diagonals, as on the corps designating flag. These measured one and one-half feet on the staff by two feet long, "with the name of the battery in black letters on the white stripe."

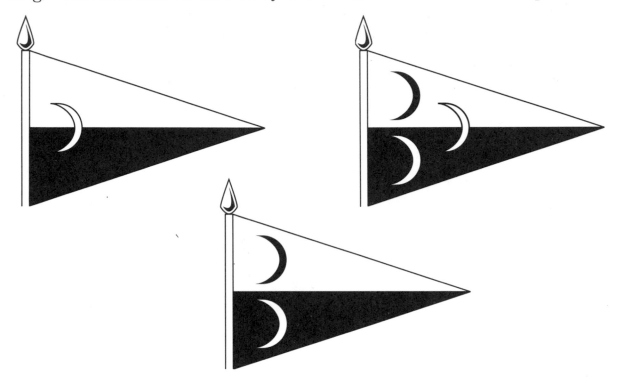

Figures 67, 68, & 69: Headquarters Flags of the
Divisions of the Reserve Corps, Army of the
Cumberland, 1863

The General Order of April 25, 1863, established for the Artillery Reserve of the Army of the Cumberland a designating flag which was, in fact, two flags to be flown one above the other on the same staff. They were bright red, each four feet wide by two feet long. The batteries of the Artillery Reserve had red flags measuring one and one-half feet wide by two feet long. Battery flags were marked "with the letters and numbers of the battery inscribed thereon, in black, 4 inches long, thus 'B, First Ohio.'"

The designating flag for the Cavalry Corps was a six-by-four-foot flag of bright blue, white, and red vertical stripes, very similar to the flag of France. The flags of the two cavalry divisions placed one or two eighteen-inch black stars, corresponding to the division's number, two inches from the staff. The brigade flags were the same design as their division's flag, with the brigade number placed on the stars, as with infantry brigades.

Figure 70: Headquarters Flag of the Cavalry Corps,
Army of the Cumberland, 1863

In the spring of 1864 the Army of the Cumberland was under the command of Maj. Gen. George H. Thomas. It was one of the two U.S. armies at Chattanooga, under the overall command of Maj. Gen. William T. Sherman. April was the lull before Sherman's storm into Georgia, and Thomas took this opportunity to establish new designating flags for the Army of the Cumberland when he issued General Order No. 62 on April 26, 1864.

The Army headquarters flag was not substantially different from that adopted in December 1862. Its dimensions were changed from six feet by five feet to five feet square.

The Twenty-First Corps was replaced in the Army of the Cumberland by the Fourth Army Corps. The new flag for the Fourth Corps was red, five feet square, with a yellow fringe. On the red flag was a blue union, or canton, two feet square. A federal eagle in gold was placed on the canton.

Figure 71: Pattern for the Headquarters Flags of the
Fourth and Fourteenth Corps, Army of the
Cumberland, 1864

With the order of April 26, 1864, the Fourteenth Corps received its third set of designating flags since December 1862. The new corps headquarters flag was the same pattern as that used for the Fourth Corps, but the colors were reversed: a gold eagle in a red canton on a blue flag.

The division flags of the Fourth and Fourteenth Corps had the same color patterns as the headquarters flags of their respective corps, but without the eagle or the yellow fringe. Instead of an eagle, the divisions were designated by a system of white bars, three inches wide, placed on the canton. Each first division displayed a single white bar running from the upper right to the lower left corner of the canton. The second divisions of these corps had two bars crossing, forming a Saint Andrew's cross in the canton. The third divisions added a third bar running vertically through the center of the crossed bars, from the top to the bottom of the canton.

Figure 72: Pattern for the Brigade Flags of the Third
Divisions of the Fourth and Fourteenth Corps,
Army of the Cumberland, 1864

Designating flags for the brigades were based on the flags of their respective divisions. A swallow-tail was cut into the outer edge, the distance from the staff to the angle of the fork measuring three feet. White stars corresponding in number with the number of the brigade were placed below the canton on a line parallel to the staff.

The new flags for the Twentieth Corps were similar to the system introduced in the Army of the Potomac in 1863. Like those, the corps designating flag was a blue swallow-tail, three feet wide and six feet long, with a white Tunic cross. The red numeral "20" was placed in the center of the cross.

Figure 73: Headquarters Flag of the Twentieth Corps,
Army of the Cumberland, 1864

The division flags were six feet square with the corps badge, a star, in the center. The flag of the First Division was a red star on a white field. A white star was placed on the blue field of the Second Division's flag. The white flags used by the Third and Fourth Divisions had, respectively, blue and green stars.

Brigade flags for the Twentieth Corps were equilateral triangle, measuring six feet on each side. The color of the field and the star were the same as used on the flag of the division to which the brigade was attached. The flag of each First Brigade had no border. Each Second Brigade's flag had a six-inch wide border along the staff the same color as its star. The Third Brigade's flag had a six-inch border the same color as the star on all three sides of the flag.

The new flag of the Cavalry Corps was very similar to that authorized in 1863. Added to it were crossed sabers in yellow, "the hilt and point of sabers extending over one-half of red and blue stripes." The yellow fringe was to be four inches wide.

Figure 74: Headquarters Flag of the Cavalry Corps,
Army of the Cumberland, 1864

The cavalry division each had flags four feet wide and six feet long. Each division flag displayed crossed sabers in the center, with the division number at the point of intersection of the sabers. The flag of the First Division had a blue numeral and red sabers on a white field. The Second Division displayed a red numeral and white sabers on blue. Red numerals and blue sabers marked the white flags of the Third and Fourth Divisions. The Fourth Cavalry Division's flag was distinguished by a nine-inch yellow border around the flag.

Designating flags for brigade headquarters of the first three cavalry divisions were triangular pennants, measuring four feet on the staff and six feet on each side. The brigade flags displayed the brigade number on crossed sabers. In the First Division the First Brigade had a blue numeral at the point of intersection of red sabers on a white field. The First Brigade of the Second Division displayed a red number and white sabers on blue. The First Brigade of the Third Division was designated by a red number and blue sabers on a white flag.

The Second Brigades of each division used the same color combinations for the fields, sabers, and numerals in their flags as were used by the First Brigade of the respective divisions. The Second Brigade, in each case, added to the flag a six-inch border on the staff. In the First Division the border was blue. It was red in the Second and Third Divisions.

Each Third Brigade's designating flag had a four-inch border on all three sides of the triangle. Again, that of the Third Brigade, First Division, was blue, and red in the case of the Third Brigades of the Second and Third Divisions.

The three brigades of the Fourth Cavalry Division were assigned flags which had the same field and device colors as the flags of the other cavalry brigades. They were bordered on their three sides by a four-inch wide margin of yellow.

IV
Army of the Ohio

At the time of the Atlanta campaign, May to September 1864, the United States forces under the command of Maj. Gen. William T. Sherman included the Army of the Cumberland, the Army of the Tennessee, and the Army of the Ohio. After the fall of Atlanta, the U.S. forces were divided. Part returned to Tennessee to contest the attempt by the Confederate Army of Tennessee to liberate that state. The Army of the Ohio occupied the city of Decatur, Georgia, and the remainder initiated Sherman's infamous march to the sea.

At the time, the Army of the Ohio was composed only of the Twenty-Third Army Corps. On September 25, 1864, Brig. Gen. J. D. Cox, in temporary command of that army, issued Special Field Orders No. 121. That order established a badge and designating flags for the Twenty-Third Corps.

The headquarters flag of the Twenty-Third Corps was a blue flag, six feet wide and six and one-half feet in length, and fringed. The corps badge, an "heraldic shield" was placed in the center. The shield was divided into three panels, the shield itself and each of the panels being outlined in gold. The upper left panel was red, the upper right, white, and the lower panel, blue.

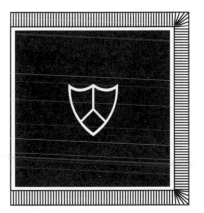

Figure 75: Headquarters Flag of the Twenty-Third
Corps, Army of the Ohio, 1864 to 1865

The division flags were smaller than the corps flag, but were also blue and fringed. Each displayed the corps shield with its three sections. The sections of the shields in the division flags, however, were not tricolored. Each was made of the same color, with the colors used to distinguish the divisions. The shield of the First Division's flag was red. The Second Division had a white shield, and that of the Third Division was blue.

Figure 76: Pattern of the Division Headquarters Flags
of the Twenty-Third Corps, Army of the Ohio, 1864

The headquarters flags for the brigades were to be "similar to the division flag, but with smaller shields along the inner margin corresponding in number to the number of the brigade."

Shortly after these flags were adopted for the Twenty-Third Corps, the Army of the Ohio was on its way back to Tennessee. It opposed the march of the Confederate Army of Tennessee, under the command of Gen. John Bell Hood, from Alabama into Tennessee, through Columbia and Springhill, to the blood-bath at Franklin, and the final repulse of the Army of Tennessee at Nashville in December 1864.

8
Naval Flags

Navies have their own specific flag terminology. Some familiarity with that terminology will help the reader better to understand this chapter.

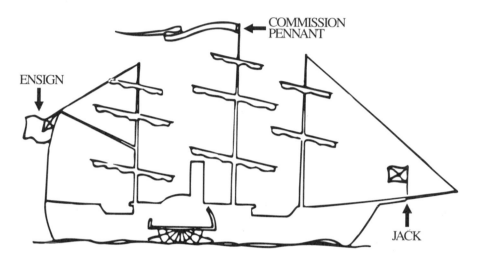

Figure 77: Illustration of a Three-Masted Ship
Demonstrating the Placement of the Ensign, Jack,
and Commission Pennant

An *ensign* is the national flag flown on a boat or ship. It is normally flown at the stern of the vessel, as shown in the accompanying illustration. On special occasion a ship will be "dressed," meaning that it will be decorated with a number of national and signal flags (and in the nineteenth century often with the ensigns and jacks of other nations. Most naval vessels carried a complete set of the ensigns, jacks, and pennants of the major naval powers.) At such times the ensign might be displayed at other masts.

It is the custom of some governments that the ensign be of a pattern different from the national flag as used on land. Such is the case with Great Britain. Its national flag is the famous "Union Jack." At sea, however, the national flag merely forms a canton on the ensign. The British Navy Ensign is a white flag with a red Cross of Saint George, and the Union Jack in the upper staff corner.

As discussed in Chapter 1, the flag of the United States evolved from the red British Naval Ensign used in the eighteenth century. For many years the "Stars and Stripes" were considered primarily a maritime flag. As a result, in America the national flag used on land and the naval ensign are of the same pattern.

The other distinctive naval flags are the jack and the commission pennant. The jack is a flag designating the nationality of the ship, which is flown from the jack staff at the bow of the ship. It is flown only on a ship of war and then only when the vessel is in port or in need of a pilot to guide it into or out of the port. The Royal Navy flies the canton of its ensign as a jack, which tradition was carried over into the United States Navy.

The commission pennant is flown from the main mast of a ship and designates its status as a commissioned vessel of its government's navy. This pennant may only be displayed by a ship in the government service.

I
The National Ensign

The ensign of the United States, whether used in the Naval Service or by merchant vessels, is the flag of the United States with the appropriate number of stars for the time period in question. The United States Navy Regulations in force during the time of the war against the Confederate States provided that ships of the several classes were to be provided with a number of flags of various sizes. These regulations established fourteen different sizes for ensigns, ranging in size from nineteen feet by thirty-six feet for the Number 1 Ensign to two and one-half feet by five feet for the Number 14 Ensign. A complete list of dimensions for ensigns, pennants, jacks, and other naval flags is set out in the appendices.

Figure 78: United States Navy "Boat Flag"

FLAGS OF THE UNION

The ensigns designated numbers 10 through 14 were for boats (as opposed to ships) and were often referred to as "boat flags." It was a common tradition, though apparently not officially sanctioned by the 1863 Navy Regulations, for boat flags to have only thirteen stars.

II
The Union Jack

The term *Union Jack* most often calls to mind the flag of Great Britain, which is commonly called by that name. The more appropriate name for the British banner is the *Union Flag*, representing the union of England, Scotland, and Ireland, and being in fact a union of three flags representing those countries. Because it serves as the Royal Navy's jack, however, it has come to be called the Union Jack.

In the United States Navy the jack is also the canton, or union, of the ensign, and in the naval service the name used for the United States Navy's jack is also the Union Jack. It is a plain blue flag with one star for each state in the Union.

Figure 79: United States Navy Jack, 1861 to 1863

Navy Regulations of the period specified that jacks were "to be the same as the union separated from the rest of the ensign; when hoisted at the fore it is a signal for a pilot." The regulations provided for eight sizes of jacks which were to be matched with the corresponding number of ensign; that is, when a Number 1 Ensign was being flown, the appropriate jack to use was the Number 1 Jack. The Number 1 Jack measured ten and one-quarter feet wide by fourteen and two-fifths feet long, which corresponded exactly to the size of the union of the Number 1 Ensign.

III
The Commission Pennant

Navy commission pennants are designed to indicate the nationality of a ship and its commissioned status in the government service. In the past it was also referred to as the "narrow pennant" to distinguish it from the "broad pennant," which will be discussed shortly.

Figure 80: United States Navy Commission Pennant

Navy Regulations provided that the narrow pennant was to have "the union part composed of thirteen white stars in a horizontal line, on a blue field, one-fourth the length of the pennant, the remaining three-fourths of its length to be of a red and white stripe, of the same breadth at any part of the taper, with the red uppermost. The number of stars in the union part of night and boat pennants to be confined to seven."

As with the jack, regulations prescribed eight different sizes of commission pennants, corresponding to the first eight ensigns authorized. The Number 1 Narrow Pennant, to be flown with the Number 1 Ensign, was 52/100ths of a foot wide (about six and one-fourth inches) and seventy feet long.

IV
Officers' Flags

Distinctive flags were prescribed to be flown from a mast of the ship commanded by the officer commanding a fleet or a squadron. It is from this that the term "flag ship" is derived.

The flag of an admiral commanding a fleet was to be a plain rectangular flag, colored either blue, red, or white. The color indicated the grade of the admiral, blue being the senior rank and white the most junior grade.

The flag of a commodore, flown when he was in command of a squadron, or when duly authorized to hoist it at a naval station, was referred to as the "broad pennant." While the commission or "narrow" pennant was long and thin, the commodore's pennant was short, much wider than the commission pennant, and swallow-tailed.

Figure 81: Commodore's Broad Pennant

Regulations specified that the lower edge of the commodore's pennant was to be at a right angle to the hoist, "but, on the contrary, the upper side is to be sloped, and so as to narrow the pennant across at the extremity of the tails one-tenth the measure of the hoist, and thus render the upper tail correspondingly shorter than the lower one." As with the admirals' flags, the broad pennants were either blue, red, or white, depending upon the commodore's seniority of rank. The pennants also displayed stars "equal to the number of States, and which are to be white in the blue and red pennants, and blue in the white pennant." The angle of the swallow-tail was to begin at a point three-fifths the length of the pennant from the hoist.

Regulations also established eight numbered sizes for these flags. A Number 1 Admiral's Distinctive Flag measured ten and one-quarter feet wide by fourteen and four-tenths feet long. A Number 1 Commodore's Broad Pennant measured ten and four-fifths feet wide by eighteen feet long.

V
Signal Flags

In the 1860s the United States Navy used two different systems of signal flags. It is beyond the scope of this book to delve deeply into the complications of naval signal flags, but there were a few signal flags with constant and readily recognized meanings which we will illustrate.

Figure 82: Guard Signal

Among the rectangular signal flags used by the navy was one displaying a red saltier or Cross of Saint Andrew on a white field. It was designated the "guard" signal. As such, it was flown by the ship in a fleet or squadron with which all approaching vessels had to register.

Figure 83: Church Pennant

The church pennant, featuring a blue cross on a white field, indicated that worship services were being conducted on the vessel at the time it was displayed. The church pennant was flown at the same place as, and above, the national ensign. It was the only flag of any kind that was ever allowed to fly above the ensign.

The yellow flag was flown at the foremast of any vessel placed in quarantine. Because quarantine was often associated with the presence on board of a communicable disease, the yellow flag became associated with the medical service. Hence its introduction into the army as a hospital flag.

Navy Regulations specified the number and size of signal flags to be allotted to and flown by naval vessels. A Number 1 Guard Signal was eleven feet by thirteen feet. A Number 1 Church Pennant was five and one-half feet wide and twenty-four feet long to its point. A Number 1 Quarantine Flag was nine feet wide and eleven feet long.

VI
Foreign Flags

Every seagoing vessel of the United States Navy was issued a number of complete sets of foreign flags. These sets included not only the ensign, but also the narrow pennant and jack for each government represented. It was common practice to fly from the foremast the ensign of a nation whose port was being visited. This was known as a "courtesy flag." The reason to have complete sets of ensigns, pennants, and jacks, however, was to be able to fly them as a *ruse de guerre*, to fool an enemy. In such an event, the proper colors were supposed to be raised once an engagement commenced.

When the United States naval facilities at Norfolk, Virginia, fell to Virginia authorities in 1861, among the naval stores accounted for were a number of complete sets of foreign flags representing thirty-nine nations. This shows that United States war ships were apparently supplied with flags for virtually every maritime power of any significance at the time.

VII
Distribution of Flags to Naval Vessels

United States Navy vessels intended for service on the high seas were grouped into four ratings. Ships of the first rate were the largest and most heavily armed; those of the fourth rate were the lightest vessels for sea service. The number and size of flags supplied to each vessel depended upon its rating. For example, ships of the first rate were the only ships issued Number 1 Ensigns and the corresponding pennants and other flags. The largest flags for ships of the second rate were Number 2; Number 3 for ships of the third rate; and Number 4 for ships of the fourth rate.

Seagoing vessels were each distributed a set of foreign flags corresponding to the third size of United States flags that the vessel was authorized to carry. Therefore, first-rate ships would carry a set of foreign flags corresponding in size to the Number 3 flags. Ships of the second rate would be issued Number 4 foreign flags, and so forth.

Vessels intended for service only on the inland waters were not issued full sets of flags for their rates. They were authorized only three each of the ensign, narrow pennant, and jack. They were not issued foreign flags. Additionally, ships, whether for high seas or inland service, were only issued distinctive flags for admirals or commodores if the ship was actually intended to wear the flag in question.

9
Revenue Service Flags

In 1790 the United States acquired ten ships to patrol the Atlantic coast in an effort to stop smugglers attempting to avoid the payment of import duties. Originally called the Revenue Marines, this organization eventually evolved into the United States Coast Guard.

In 1799 the United States were engaged in an unofficial naval war with France, which called most of the navy into the high seas, away from the coast. That year the Revenue Service was officially transferred to the Treasury Department, so that the important business of collecting the tariff could continue. The law authorizing this maritime force for the Treasury Department also authorized the president to establish a flag for the ships of the Revenue Service.

Figure 84: Revenue Service Flag

The flag adopted for the Revenue Service in 1799 kept the elements of the United States flag, but radically rearranged them. The union of the flag was changed from blue to white. On the union was placed a blue federal eagle under an arch of thirteen blue stars. The most radical feature, however, was the arrangement of the stripes. The flag's sixteen stripes, corresponding in number to the States in the Union in 1799, were placed vertically across its field.

That same flag, with the addition of the Coast Guard seal in its field of stripes, is in service today as the Coast Guard ensign.

Figure 85: Revenue Service Narrow Pennant

The Revenue Service was also granted its own distinctive commission pennant. Based upon the design of the ensign, it displayed thirteen blue stars on a white union. The balance of the pennant was a series of sixteen red and white vertical stripes, terminating in a red swallow-tail. This pennant is now the commission pennant of the Coast Guard.

FLAGS OF THE UNION

Further Reading

Other books are available for further study of United States and Confederate flags, and of flags in general. A good study of the development of the United States flag during the time of the American Revolution is:

Richardson, Edward H. *Standards and Colors of the American Revolution.* Philadelphia: The University of Pennsylvania Press, 1982.

For a thoroughly detailed study of the flags used by the units of one Northern state during the War for Southern Independence see:

Sauers, Richard A. *Advance the Colors! Pennsylvania Civil War Battle Flags.* Harrisburg: The Capitol Preservation Committee, 1987.

Studies of Confederate flags may be pursued in the following works:

Cannon, Devereaux D., Jr. *The Flags of the Confederacy: An Illustrated History.* Gretna, La.: Pelican Publishing Company, 1988.

Madaus, Howard Michael. *The Battle Flags of the Confederate Army of Tennessee.* Milwaukee: Milwaukee Public Museum, 1976.

Madaus, Howard Michael. "Rebel Flags Afloat." *The Flag Bulletin*, Vol. XXV, No. 1. Winchester, Mass.: The Flag Research Center, 1986.

Madaus, Howard Michael. "Unit Colors of the Trans-Mississippi Confederacy." *Military Collector & Historian*, Vol. XLI, Nos. 3 and 4. Westbrook, Conn.: Company of Military Historians, 1989.

Some general histories of state flags that include the period of the War for Southern Independence include:

Cannon, Devereaux D., Jr. *Flags of Tennessee.* Gretna, La.: Pelican Publishing Company, 1991.

Gilbert, Charles E., Jr. *Flags of Texas.* Gretna, La.: Pelican Publishing Company, 1989.

For general works on flags the reader may refer to a large number of sources. Two of those have been written by the director of the Flag Research Center:

Smith, Whitney. *The Flag Book of the United States.* New York: William Morrow & Company, Inc., 1970.

Smith, Whitney. *Flags Through the Ages and Across the World.* New York: McGraw-Hill, 1975.

The Flag Research Center publishes a bimonthly journal called *The Flag Bulletin.* It is available from the Flag Research Center, 3 Edgehill Road, Winchester, Massachusetts 01890.

Appendix A
United States Flag Laws

I
FLAG RESOLUTION OF 1777

Resolved, that the flag of the thirteen United States be 13 stripes alternate red and white: that the union be 13 stars, white, in a blue field, representing a new constellation.

Passed June 14, 1777.

II
FLAG ACT OF 1794

Be it enacted by the Senate and House of Representatives of the United States of America in Congress assembled, That from and after the first day of May anno Domini one thousand seven hundred and ninety-five, the flag of the United States, be fifteen stripes alternate red and white. That the Union be fifteen stars, white in a blue field.

Approved, January 13, 1794.

III
FLAG ACT OF 1818

Sect. 1. *Be it enacted by the Senate and House of Representatives of the United States of America in Congress assembled,* That from and after the fourth day of July next, the flag of the United States be thirteen horizontal stripes, alternate red and white; that the union have twenty stars, white in a blue field.

Sect. 2. *And be it further enacted,* That on the admission of every State into the Union, one star be added to the union of the flag; and that such addition shall take effect on the fourth day of July next succeeding such admission.

Approved, April 4, 1818.

Appendix B
Revised Regulations for the Army
of the United States, 1861

ARTICLE L.
FLAGS, COLORS, STANDARDS, GUIDONS.

Garrison Flag.

1436. The garrison flag is the national flag. It is made of bunting, thirty-six feet fly, and twenty feet hoist, in thirteen horizontal stripes of equal breadth, alternately red and white, beginning with the red. In the upper quarter, next the staff, is the Union, composed of a number of white stars, equal to the number of the States, on a blue field, one-third the length of the flag, extending to the lower edge of the fourth red stripe from the top. The storm flag is twenty feet by ten feet; the recruiting flag, nine feet nine inches by four feet four inches.

Colors of Artillery Regiments.

1437. Each regiment of Artillery shall have two silken colors. The first, or the national color, of stars and stripes, as described for the garrison flag. The number and name of the regiment to be embroidered with gold on the centre stripe. The second, or regimental color, to be yellow, of the same dimensions as the first, bearing in the centre two cannon crossing, with the letters U.S. above, and the number of the regiment below; fringe, yellow. Each color to be six feet six inches fly, and six feet deep on the pike. The pike, including the spear and ferrule, to be nine feet ten inches in length. Cords and tassels, red and yellow silk, intermixed.

Colors of Infantry Regiments.

1438. Each regiment of Infantry shall have two silken colors. The first, or the national color, of stars and stripes, as described for the garrison flag. The number and name of the regiment to be embroidered with silver on the centre stripe. The second, or regimental color, to be blue, with the arms of the United States embroidered in silk on the centre. The name of the regiment in a scroll, underneath the eagle. Each color to be six feet six inches fly, and six feet deep on the pike. The length of the pike, including the spear and ferrule, to be nine feet ten inches in length. The fringe yellow; cords and tassels, blue and white silk intermixed.

Camp Colors.

1439. The camp colors are of bunting, eighteen inches square; white for infantry, and red for artillery, with the number of the regiment on them. The pole eight feet long.

Standards and Guidons
for Mounted Regiments.

1440. Each regiment will have a silken standard, and each company a silken guidon. The standard to bear the arms of the United States, embroidered in silk, on a blue ground, with the number and name of the regiment, in a scroll underneath the eagle. The flag of the standard to be two feet five inches wide, and two feet three inches on the lance, and to be edged with yellow silk fringe.

1441. The flag of the guidon is swallow-tailed, three feet five inches from the lance to the end of the swallow-tail; fifteen inches to the fork of the swallow-tail, and two feet three inches on the lance. To be half red and half white, dividing at the fork, the red above. On the red, the letters U.S. in white; and on the white, the letter of the company in red. The lance of the standards and guidons to be nine feet long, including spear and ferrule.

Appendix C

GENERAL ORDERS }
    No. 4   }

HEADQUARTERS OF THE ARMY,
ADJUTANT GENERAL'S OFFICE,
Washington, January 18, 1862.

I. Under instructions from the Secretary of War, dated January 7, 1862, guidons and camp colors for the Army will be made like the United States flag, with stars and stripes.

. . .

By command of Major-General McClellan:

L. THOMAS
Adjutant-General

Appendix D
Dimensions of Navy Ensigns, Pennants, Jacks, Etc.

ENSIGNS
[Dimensions in Feet]

Number	Hoist	Length	Length of Union
1	19.00	36.00	14.40
2	16.90	32.00	12.80
3	14.80	28.00	11.20
4	13.20	25.00	10.00
5	11.60	22.00	8.80
6	10.00	19.00	7.60
7	8.45	16.00	6.40
8	7.40	14.00	5.60
9	6.33	12.00	4.80
10	5.28	10.00	4.00
11	4.20	8.00	3.20
12	3.70	7.00	2.80
13	3.20	6.00	2.40
14	2.50	5.00	2.00

[Ensigns Nos. 10 through 14 are boat flags]

NARROW PENNANTS
[Dimensions in Feet]

Number	Hoist	Length	Length of Union
1	0.52	70.00	17.50
2	0.48	55.00	13.75
3	0.42	40.00	10.00
4	0.40	30.00	7.50
5	0.35	25.00	6.25
6	0.30	20.00	5.00
7	0.25	9.00	2.25
8	0.24	6.00	1.50

JACKS
[Dimensions in Feet]

Number	Hoist	Length
1	10.25	14.40
2	9.00	12.80
3	8.00	11.20
4	7.00	10.00
5	6.25	8.80
6	5.40	7.60
7	4.50	6.40
8	4.00	5.60

DISTINCTIVE FLAGS OF OFFICERS
[Dimensions in Feet]

Number	Admirals		Commodores	
	Hoist	Length	Hoist	Length
1	10.25	14.40	10.80	18.00
2	9.00	12.80	9.60	16.00
3	8.00	11.20	8.40	14.00
4	7.00	10.00	7.20	12.00
5	6.25	8.80	6.00	10.00
6	5.40	7.60	4.80	8.00
7	4.50	6.40	3.60	6.00
8	4.00	5.60	3.00	5.00

Index

Adjutant-General, 30
Admiral's Flag, 79
Alabama, 23, 62
American Party, 22
American Stripes, 19
Army of Tennessee, C.S.A., 73, 74
Army of the Cumberland, 43, 62–72, 73
Army of the James, 58–62
Army of the Ohio, 73–74
Army of the Potomac, 46–58, 59, 71
Army of the Tennessee, 73
Articles of Confederation, 19
Artillery Colors, 41–42
Artillery Guidons, 42
Attorney General, 23–24

Bedford Militia, 17
Bell, John, 22
Boston, Massachusetts, 17
Bradley, Stephen R., 20
Breckinridge, John C., 22
British Naval Ensign, 76
British Red Ensign, 17
Broad Pennant, 78, 79
Burnside, Ambrose, 52

Caesar, 46
Camp Colors, 34–35
Cavalry Corps, Army of the Cumberland, 68–69, 72
Cavalry Corps, Army of the Potomac, 58
Cavalry Division, Army of the Cumberland, 64
Cavalry Guidons, 38–39
Cavalry Standards, 37–38
Chattanooga, Tennessee, 69
Color Bearers, 32
Color Guard, 32
Color Line, 33, 35
Color Sergeants, 32
Columbia, Tennessee, 74
Commission Pennant, 75, 78
Commodore's Pennant (see also Broad Pennant), 79

Confederate States of America, 13, 23, 25, 46
Confederation Congress, 20
Congress, U.S., 20, 21, 22
Constitution, U.S., 20, 23
Constitutional Union Party, 22
Continental Army, 17, 19
Continental Congress, 17, 18, 19
Cox, J.D., 73
Crescent Moon, 53
Cross of Saint George, 75

Decatur, Georgia, 73
Democratic Party, 22
Department of the Cumberland, 62
Department of Virginia and North Carolina, 58–59
Designating Flags, 45–74
Douglas, Stephen A., 22

Eighteenth Corps, 60, 61–62
Eleventh Corps, 53, 54
Engineer Corps, Army of the Cumberland, 64

Fifth Corps, 50, 53, 54, 55
First Corps, 47, 48, 53, 54
Flag Act of 1794, 20, 87
Flag Act of 1818, 21, 87
Flag Resolution of 1777, 18–19, 87
Flag Ship, 78
Flank Markers, 35
Florida, 23
Foreign Flags, 75, 81, 82
Fort McHenry, 21
Fort Sumter, 13
Fourteenth Corps, 62, 63, 66, 67, 70
Fourth Corps, 50, 69, 70
Franklin, State of, 20
Franklin, Tennessee, 74

Garrison, 25
Garrison Flag, 25–26, 27
General Guide Markers, 35

General Order No. 4, 34, 39, 90
General Order No. 9, 43
General Order No. 13, 62
General Order No. 41, 62, 64
General Order No. 62, 69
General Order No. 91, 64, 68
General Order No. 177, 66, 67
Georgia, 23, 62, 69
Grand Union Flag, 17–18
Grant, Ulysses S., 45–46
Great Britain, 19
Greek Cross, 51

Heart, 56
Hood, John Bell, 74
Hospital Flag, 43–44, 64

Indiana, 21
Industrial Revolution, 22
Infantry Colors, 29–35
Internal Improvements, 22

Kansas, 23
Kentucky, 20
King, John H., 67
Know Nothing Party, 22

Lexington, Massachusetts, 17
Lincoln, Abraham, 22
Louisiana, 21, 23

Maltese Cross, 50, 55
Massachusetts, 20
Meade, George G., 46
Medical Service, 43–44, 64
Medical Service Guidon, 43–44
Mexican War, 22, 32
Mexico, 24
Mississippi, 23
Montgomery, Alabama, 23
Murfreesboro, Tennessee, 64

Narrow Pennant, 78
Nashville, Tennessee, 74
National Colors, 29–30, 31, 32, 35, 37, 41
National Standard, 37

Naval Ensign, 75, 76–77, 78
Naval Flags, 75–84
Naval Jack (see also Union Jack), 75, 77, 78
Nevada, 24
New Hampshire, 20
New York, 20
Nineteenth Corps, 55
Ninth Corps, 52
North Carolina, 20

Ohio, 21
Oregon, 22

Pennsylvania, 30, 37–38
Philadelphia, Pennsylvania, 19
Popular Sovereignty, 22
Prospect Hill, 17

Quarantine Flag, 43, 81
Quartermaster's Depots, 64

Recruiting Flag, 26–27
Regimental Colors, 31–32, 35, 37
Regulations, U.S. Army, 25, 26, 30, 32, 35, 39, 41, 88–89
Regulations, U.S. Navy, 76, 77, 81, 91–93
Republican Party, 22
Reserve Corps, Army of the Cumberland, 67–68
Revenue Marines, 83
Revenue Service, 83–84
Rhode Island, 20
Richmond, Virginia, 46
Rio Grande, 24
Rosecrans, William S., 62, 63, 64
Royal Navy, 76

Saint Andrew's Cross, 51, 70, 80
Saltier, 51, 80
Second Corps, 48, 50, 53
Secretary of War, 34
Shamrock, 48
Shelby, Joseph O., 24
Shepherd, Oliver L., 64
Sherman, William T., 69, 75

Shield, 52
Signal Flags, 80–81
Sixth Corps, 51, 53
Slavery, 22
Somerville, Massachusetts, 17
South Carolina, 23
Special Field Orders No. 121, 73
Springhill, Tennessee, 74
Square, 57
Stars and Stripes, 18, 29, 31, 34, 37,
    39, 41, 76
State Colors, 30
State Standard, 37–38
Storm Flag, 26, 27

Tariffs, 22
Tennessee, 21, 62
Tenth Corps, 59–61, 62
Third Corps, 49, 53
Thomas, George H., 69
Treasury Department, 83

Trefoil, 48
Tunic Cross, 47, 49, 53, 54, 71
Twelfth Corps, 54
Twentieth Corps, 64–65, 71
Twenty-Fifth Corps, 57
Twenty-First Corps, 64–65, 69
Twenty-Fourth Corps, 56
Twenty-Third Corps, 73–74

Union Jack (see also Naval Jack), 75, 77
United States Coast Guard, 83, 84

Vermont, 20
Virginia, 20, 23–24, 46

War Department, 30, 43
Washington, George, 17, 19
Waud, A.R., 46
West Virginia, 23–24
Whig Party, 22